How to Handle Bullying and Gangs

UNDER PRESSURE

How to Handle Bullying and Gangs

by Honor Head

Smart Apple Media

Published in 2015 in the United States by Smart Apple Media, an imprint of Black Rabbit Books

Smart Apple Media
PO Box 3263, Mankato, Minnesota 56002

Copyright © Arcturus Holdings Limited

Editors: Rachel Minay and Joe Harris
Design: Emma Randall
Cover design: Emma Randall

Picture Credits
Shutterstock: cover (Morgar), 1 (pjcross), 4 (Pressmaster), 5 (Roxana Gonzalez), 6 (Monkey Business Images), 7 (Lisa S.), 8 (Goodluz), 9 (funflow), 10 (ejwhite), 11 (michaeljung), 12 (Christy Thompson), 13 (Petrenko Andriy), 14 (Andrey_Popov), 15 (Monkey Business Images), 16 (Pressmaster), 17 (grafvision), 18 (Albo), 19 (William Perugini), 20 (racorn), 21, 22 (Monkey Business Images), 23 (Oleg_Mit), 24 (Vitalinka), 25 (bikeriderlondon), 26 (Monkey Business Images), 27 (Elena Elisseeva), 28 (michaeljung), 29 (Tad Denson), 30 (auremar), 31 (auremar), 32 (wavebreakmedia), 33 (Eugenia-Petrenko), 34 (muzsy), 35 (RyFlip), 36 (ffolas), 37 (CREATISTA), 38 (raluca teodorescu), 39 (Ljupco Smokovski), 40 (Rob Marmion), 41 (hartphotography).

Library of Congress Cataloging-in-Publication Data

Head, Honor.
 How to handle bullying and gangs / Honor Head.
    pages cm. -- (Under pressure)
Includes index.
ISBN 978-1-59920-825-1
1. Bullying--Juvenile literature. 2. Aggressiveness in adolescence--Juvenile literature. 3. Gangs--Juvenile literature. 4. Peer pressure--Juvenile literature. I. Title.
 BF637.B85H43 2015
 302.34'3--dc23

                    2013047542

Printed in China

SL004070US

Supplier 29, Date 0514, Print Run 3390

987654321

CONTENTS

WHAT ARE BULLYING AND GANGS?

Bullying is when someone deliberately and repeatedly hurts, **humiliates,** or threatens another person. Bullying can take place in school, online, in the street, or at home. It can make the person being bullied feel very alone and seriously affect his or her self-confidence.

A "gang" of friends that look out for one another is a good thing, but some gangs are just looking for trouble.

WHAT IS BULLYING?

Bullying is when someone says or does something nasty to you more than once. It is repeated name-calling, hurting, or threatening. If you are being bullied, it is not your fault. Bullying is wrong, and you don't have to put up with it. If you are a bully or part of a gang that is bullying, you need to face up to what you are doing and change your behavior.

TYPES OF BULLYING

There are three types of bullying. Verbal bullying is saying or writing mean things, name-calling, or nasty threats. Social bullying is spreading rumors, leaving someone out of activities on purpose, or embarrassing him or her in front of others. Physical bullying includes hitting, spitting, damaging someone's belongings, and making rude gestures.

IS A GANG ALWAYS BAD?

A "gang" has different meanings. A gang might just be a group of friends who like to hang out together, and this is fine, but some **antisocial** gangs might bully or threaten others. Some gangs are involved with violence and crime. These gangs usually have adult members but may try to involve younger people in the gang.

There are lots of helplines and organizations that give help and advice about being bullied.

"Bullied by my ex-best friend"

I was getting bullied by my ex-best friend. We used to do everything together, but then she started being best friends with someone else and started calling me names and saying nasty things about me. I didn't think I was the sort of person who would be bullied, but now I know it can happen to anyone. I am learning to deal with it, and now I have another best friend, but it was very hurtful to have my best friend turn on me.

BULLYING

Bullying can happen to anyone. It can take many forms, from name-calling to physically hurting someone. Being ignored or left out by friends is also a form of bullying. Bullying can happen for a short period of time or over a very long time.

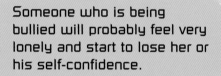

Someone who is being bullied will probably feel very lonely and start to lose her or his self-confidence.

FEELING BAD

Bullying makes people feel unhappy, lonely, and scared, and it can lead to dangerous and harmful behavior. People who are the target of bullying often start to feel worthless. In some cases, this lack of **self-esteem** can last into adulthood, and it can make it difficult for them to form happy relationships or build successful careers.

PICKING SOMEONE OUT

Bullies will find whatever hurts or upsets someone the most. Bullies might pick a target for his or her race, disability, looks, sexual preferences, or good or bad grades at school. Some bullies might pick on one thing that makes a person stand out—maybe a hobby, something about their home life, or even what they wear.

Bullies might threaten people into doing something illegal such as shoplifting. This can get the person being bullied into serious trouble.

Under Pressure Q&A

GETTING WORSE

Physical bullying can begin with pushing and shoving, and this can soon grow into beating someone up. Bullies might try to grab someone's bag or belongings, tear or dirty his or her clothes, or force him or her to hand over lunch money or other possessions.

ILLEGAL AND DANGEROUS

Some bullies might try and make you do things you don't want to, such as shoplifting or stealing from classmates. Some gangs make new members do **illegal** or dangerous things to prove they are loyal to the gang.

Is this bullying?

I've just started going to a new school, and no one is really nasty to me, but no one asks me to do any stuff with them or sits with me at lunch. When I try to speak to them, they say things about being a newbie and that they already have friends. I feel very lonely. Mom says it will get better, but I'm not sure. Is this bullying? What should I do?

It could be the people at your new school need time to get to know you, but it could be a form of bullying—deliberately leaving a person out of activities and isolating him or her. It is difficult when you want to be part of a group, but try not to seem too pushy. Be polite and friendly, but maybe stand back a little and let them come to you. Is there an after-school group you can join so you have some friends elsewhere, for instance, a book or movie club, or a sports or dance club? That way, you'll meet lots of different people.

CYBERBULLYING

Social media is great for keeping in touch with your friends and finding out what's going on. However, it can also be used for cyberbullying on cell phones, email, or through chat rooms and instant messaging—anything that is done digitally. It is easy to bully someone online because it can be done **anonymously** from anywhere. Cyberbullying can be very scary, but you can take action to stop it.

Never forward a nasty email, text message, or instant message as this makes you part of the cyberbullying.

WHAT IS CYBERBULLYING?

Forms of cyberbullying include using text messages, emails, social networking sites, instant messaging, and chat rooms to threaten or humiliate someone and to post rumors, lies, or embarrassing photos. Cyberbullying is an ongoing attack by one or more people to cause distress or to isolate someone digitally.

NOWHERE IS SAFE

Cyberbullying can happen anywhere. Even home is not a safe place. A person can be cyberbullied on the weekends, on vacation, and even in the middle of the night. Good social media sites and cell providers take cyberbullying very seriously and have special help desks that give advice about cyberbullying.

Check your privacy settings on social media sites to make sure you have the highest privacy possible. This will help to stop bullies from getting through.

JUST A JOKE?

Some people who send nasty messages or post embarrassing pictures anonymously might think it is just a joke, but it isn't funny for the person at the other end. If you have done this, think about how you would feel if someone did it to you.

BLOCK AND STOP

If you are being cyberbullied, never reply to a bullying message or respond if something nasty is uploaded about you. This will encourage the bully. Keep anything you receive as evidence to show an adult. You can stop messages getting through by blocking the email address and cell phone number they come from and deleting the bully from your social media contacts.

Under Pressure Q&A

How can I stop the horrible text messages?

I keep getting nasty text messages on my cell day and night. I need my phone to keep in touch with my friends, but these messages really frighten me and they're getting worse. What can I do?

Don't ignore it. Try not to delete the messages, but show them to an adult you trust, at home or at school, so they can report it to the phone company. Do not reply to the messages because this will encourage the person to send even more. Block the number the calls are coming from, or change your number and only give your new one to people you really trust.

WHY DO PEOPLE BECOME BULLIES?

Sometimes, understanding why people become bullies can help you to deal with bullying. However, there are many possible reasons, and you may never know why someone has become a bully or why they have chosen their target. The main thing to remember is that bullying is wrong, and the person being bullied is not to blame.

COWARDLY AND INSECURE

Bullies are often cowardly and insecure themselves. Maybe they feel that they could be a target of bullying, so they hide their fear or feeling of being **inadequate** by trying to control others.

A BULLYING BACKGROUND

Some bullies may be bullied themselves at home by an older sibling or a parent, or they may come from a family where there is not much love or caring. In some families, name-calling, rough behavior, and even violence happens every day.

If there is a lot of shouting or bullying at home, some people continue this behavior at school.

POWER PLAY

Some people like the power they feel through bullying. They think that people look up to them and think they're cool. Usually people fear and despise bullies but are too frightened to say so.

SEEKING ATTENTION OR BLENDING IN

Some young people just want the attention they get as bullies. Some may join in with bullying because they want to be part of the group. Or if they are in a gang, the other members may have put pressure on them to bully, too.

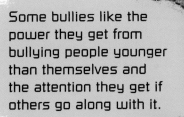

Some bullies like the power they get from bullying people younger than themselves and the attention they get if others go along with it.

"I felt angry all the time"

I started picking on boys smaller than me in my first year of middle school. At first, it was just for fun, but then I thought, "Oh, this makes me feel good." My dad was giving me a hard time at home, and I felt angry all the time. After a while, I noticed people tried to avoid me, so I asked my best friend what was going on. He was a little nervous but said that everybody was scared of me and didn't like that I bullied the smaller kids. I thought we were all just having fun, but my friend said that they were going along with me because they thought I might pick on them next. My homeroom teacher spoke to me about seeing a counselor. I wasn't sure I wanted to talk to someone, but he was great. We talked a lot about how angry I felt toward my dad and that bullying was my way of getting back some control over my life. I don't want to be a horrible bully like my dad, and now my counselor is helping me to figure it all out.

WHO GETS BULLIED?

Bullying can happen to anyone, but no one deserves to be bullied, and there is never a reason or excuse for it. Some young people are bullied because they are different in some way. This bullying may be the result of **prejudice**: This is when someone forms an opinion about another person or group of people based on fear, hatred, or ignorance.

Everyone has their own beliefs and way of living. No one should be bullied for being different.

RACE AND RELIGION

Whatever their culture or faith, everyone should be respected for their beliefs and the way they choose to live. If you are being called names or threatened because of your race, accent, religion, or color, this may be **racist** abuse and it could be against the law. Tell a teacher or trusted adult what is happening.

HOMOPHOBIC BULLYING

Homophobic bullying happens when others think someone may be gay, lesbian, bisexual, or **transgender**, or perhaps because he or she lives with parents of the same sex. This bullying is based on prejudice. If the bullies follow you home, threaten you in the street, or attack you, it is called a **hate crime** and should be reported to the police.

Even if bullying happens on weekends, if the bullies are from the same school as the person they're targeting, the school should be told.

THE RIGHT TO FEEL SAFE

Sometimes people are bullied just because they are different in some way—this could be anything from wearing different clothes to having a learning disability. However, some people will never know why they are being bullied. If you are being bullied, remember that you have the **right** to feel safe wherever you are, both mentally and physically.

TELL SOMEONE

It can be very hard to report bullying. It may seem that you are "**snitching**" on someone, but as well as keeping yourself safe, you could be saving someone else from getting hurt by stopping the bully. Talk to someone in confidence about what is going on, or phone a helpline and talk through what your options are.

Under Pressure Q&A

Should I ignore this bullying?

I'm being bullied because I'm a Christian. It's not much, just name-calling, but it upsets me. I don't want to bother my family with it because it will upset them, too. Should I just ignore it?

Everyone has the right to live according to their own beliefs and choices. What you are experiencing is a form of prejudice and religious harassment, and you mustn't let it go on. Keep a record of who says what to you, where, and when, and report it to a teacher or school counselor. Tell your parents—they will be more upset to think you didn't go to them for help.

WHAT IT FEELS LIKE TO BE BULLIED

Are you putting up with name-calling or people whispering behind your back? Perhaps you are being left out of what's going on, being pushed around, knocked down, or laughed at? If so, you may be feeling miserable, angry, and worthless, and dread going to school.

Someone who is being bullied often feels very alone, even when she or he is with family or friends.

ISOLATION

People who are bullied can soon become isolated and lonely. Maybe their best friends have turned on them or become **bystanders**, or they are no longer included in social activities. Often people do not want to be seen with a victim of bullying. The young person who is being bullied will probably start to hate going to school.

FEELING WORTHLESS

Most people who are being bullied say that they begin to feel worthless. They lose their self-esteem and self-respect. They often think they are powerless, alone, and unpopular, and they may feel as if no one cares whether they live or die. These feelings can lead to **depression** and **reckless** or harmful behavior.

Someone being bullied may spend a lot of time in their room, feeling sad, lonely, and ashamed.

SELF-HARMING AND SUICIDE

Some people who have been badly bullied for a long time might start to self-harm. This is when they cut themselves with a razor or knife, burn themselves, or harm themselves in some other way. Some start pulling out their hair. Life can become so miserable, frightening, and lonely that in extreme cases, they may even think about committing suicide, especially if they're not getting any support at home.

BE BRAVE AND BELIEVE

If you are being bullied, you must remember that you are a good, strong, and special person. If you feel worthless, that's because this is what the bully wants you to feel, not because that's what you are. Be brave and take the first steps to making yourself feel good again—phone a helpline or talk to someone you trust. You can make the bullying stop.

"I thought it must be my fault"

I was beaten up almost every day after school and called names. I cried myself to sleep every night. I was ashamed to tell my mom because I thought it must be something to do with me. Then I read online about how this had happened to other people and that you shouldn't let the bullies win. I told my mom and she totally understood and talked to the principal. I was moved to another classroom, the bullies soon forgot about me, and I'm OK now. It was scary telling Mom, but I'm glad I did.

BE ASSERTIVE

If you're being bullied, it is not your fault and the bullying has to stop. Show the bullies that you are not going to put up with their nastiness anymore. Practice being **assertive**, walking tall, and looking strong.

BODY LANGUAGE

Bullies like to pick on someone who looks weak and unable to stand up for him or herself. Don't be that person. Remember to stand up straight, walk tall, keep your head up, and look strong. Even though you may be feeling nervous or **anxious**, others will think twice before picking on you.

PASSIVE BEHAVIOR

There are three basic ways you can behave around other people. One is to be **passive**. This is when someone acts as though other people have more rights than him or her and so gives in to what other people want. Don't be passive—stand up for your right to be safe, whatever you are doing.

Bullies are less likely to pick on someone who looks confident and assertive.

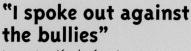

AGGRESSIVE BEHAVIOR

Behaving in an **aggressive** way is the other extreme—this is how a bully would behave. Aggressive people believe that their rights matter more than anyone else's and they should get whatever they want even if it means they have to hurt someone.

BEING ASSERTIVE

The best way to behave is to be assertive. This is when someone acts in a confident and firm way. An assertive person will stand up for his or her rights—but not in an aggressive or nasty way. Start to be assertive.

"I spoke out against the bullies"

I was terrified of going to school, terrified of walking home. A gang of bullies called me names and prodded and pushed me and tried to trip me and grab my bag and stuff like that ... it was awful. But then I thought, "I don't deserve to be bullied. Who do they think they are?" I told one bully to leave me alone or I would tell a teacher. He laughed and said he'd get me if I did. I felt really scared, but I told the teacher and she started to sort it all out. My parents had to come to school, and I felt guilty about dragging them into it, but they said they were proud that I had spoken out. At first, the bully denied it all and said I was a troublemaker, but then he actually said he was sorry! I also stood up to the other bullies, and then they all left me alone. I've now been bully-free for a year. So don't give up. Remember, just because they don't see you as a cool person, doesn't mean you aren't one.

Aggressive behavior includes finger pointing, shouting in someone's face, and threatening him or her with violence.

TAKE BACK YOUR POWER

Everyone should learn to be assertive. If you are being bullied, stand up for yourself and take back your power. You can change the way you think and start to respect yourself. Remember that you are an important person with lots to give. Believe in your ability to make things change.

IGNORE AND REJECT

It's really hard, but try to ignore the nasty remarks bullies say or write about you. You know you are not the things they call you. If they confront you, say something like: "Just go away and leave me alone," in a firm voice, then walk away. Ignore their behavior and you will be no fun to bully.

JUST SAY "NO!"

If bullies start to push or shove you, say "No!" in a firm, loud voice. Don't fight back or argue with the bullies, just walk away. Look brave even if you don't feel it. If bullies see that they cannot scare you (even though you may feel frightened), they'll usually get bored.

Looking in the mirror every morning and saying something like, "I am special" or "I am strong" can help a person raise his or her self-esteem.

Ignoring bullies and walking away from them looking confident gives them the message that they are wasting their time.

BE TRUE TO YOURSELF

If the bullies make personal comments about, for instance, the way you dress, your beliefs, or activities you like doing, try to ignore them. If you change the way you look or behave to stop the bullies, then they will have won. Remember that you have every right to be the way you are and to be treated with respect.

Under Pressure Q&A

Should I stand up for myself?

Some kids at school are making my life miserable. They keep grabbing my purse, pulling my hair, and tripping me. My friend says I've got to stand up for myself, but I'm not sure how. I don't want to get into trouble.

It's good that you have a friend to help you. It is hard to say no to bullies, but bullies are often cowards, and if you stand up to them, they may stop. Don't shout or be nasty, just say firmly that they must leave you alone or you will tell your teacher or a school counselor. If they try to physically harm you or take your belongings, say "Stop that!" in a firm voice and look them in the eye. Ask your friends to walk with you. If the bullies see you're not alone and you are being assertive, they will probably back off. If their aggressive behavior doesn't stop, you should tell a teacher.

BULLYING AT SCHOOL

PACER's National Bullying Prevention Center reports that 27 percent of children and young people say that they have been bullied at school. All schools should have an antibullying policy with rules and **procedures** to support those being bullied and help make sure school is a safe place to study and learn.

Going along with someone who is being bullied when he or she tells a teacher can help that person to feel less embarrassed or nervous about it.

AVOID THE BULLIES

If you are being bullied, talk to a teacher or school counselor. If you can, avoid the places where the bullies usually approach you. Try to be around other people if bullies are lurking—ideally within eyesight of an adult.

HELP AND TALK

Keep your eyes open for people being bullied. Talk to them, even if they are in a different grade. It always helps to know someone understands what you're going through and is on your side.

The school's antibullying policy should be easy for everyone to find, for instance, on a bulletin board and on the school's website.

ANTIBULLYING POLICY

It is useful for everyone to know what the school antibullying policy is. It should lay out some clear rules about what is unacceptable behavior. The policy should state what kind of behavior counts as bullying, so that bullies have no doubt that what they're doing is wrong.

HOW TO USE THE POLICY

The antibullying policy should also set out clear procedures for how people can report bullying. This helps those being bullied if they are not sure how to start telling someone. If you don't think the current school policy is good enough, get a group together to discuss with a teacher how you can make it work better.

"We changed the antibullying policy"

I was being bullied, so I spoke to a teacher about the antibullying policy. It didn't seem to be working because lots of kids were getting bullied and not telling anyone, so we got a group of us together and changed some things. We made sure that everyone knew their rights and that they knew exactly what was bullying and what wasn't. We also made sure they knew that if they told a teacher, they would get lots of help. Some of us who had been bullied formed our own support group. Then we talked about it at the school assembly in front of everyone. There are still some bullies at school, but I think now that the kids know what to do if they are bullied, and they feel that they have more support.

BULLYING OUTSIDE OF SCHOOL

Most bullying happens at school, but it can also happen in the street, at the playground, at bus stops, and traveling to and from school.

TRAVEL WITH A FRIEND

If you are being bullied on the way to or from school by someone from your school, you should tell a teacher or school counselor. If you can, travel with a friend or see if you can share a ride with a trusted neighbor or family friends who might be driving your way to work at the same time.

STREET GANGS

Sometimes gangs hang around and **intimidate** people in the street by calling them names, making rude gestures, using threatening language, or throwing things. These gangs can get violent, so don't confront them or get into a fight with them. Try to avoid them or ignore them. Then tell an adult, who can decide if it is a matter for the police.

It can be dangerous to try and stand up to street gangs, especially if they've been drinking alcohol. It's best to walk away and tell an adult.

GATHER EVIDENCE

If you are being harassed or bullied in the street, make a note of when it happens and at what time, so you have a record to give the police. Try to remember what the bullies looked like and what they were wearing. However, don't try to photograph them—even secretly—since this could give them an excuse to attack you.

Under Pressure Q&A

What if the bullying is outside of school?

I have just started going to watch a local football team that I really like, but some of the other boys keep tripping me and pushing me as they run past. At first, I thought it was an accident, but now they stop and call me names and laugh when I fall down. I would know what do to if I was being bullied at school, but I don't know how to handle this.

Bullying can take place outside of school. It sounds like they're trying to show the "new boy" that they're in charge, but you should not let anyone bully you or make fun of you. Tell your coach or referee or another adult at the game. If the bullies go to your school, speak to a teacher about it.

If you see a gang ahead of you and they look threatening, try and take a different route. If they are really aggressive, find a safe place, such as a library, store, or bank, and ask someone who works there to call the police.

BULLYING AT HOME

For most people, home is a safe place to live and be with the most important people in your life—your family. For some, it can be a place of fear and dread. All types of families can have problems with bullying, but no one should have to live with violence at home.

Family circumstances can change and you might get new family members, but old or new, a family should look out for each other.

SAFE AND SECURE

Families are all very different. A family might have two parents, a single parent, lots of brothers and sisters, only one child, or same-sex parents. If parents have divorced, the children might be living in a **stepfamily**. Some young people live with a **foster family**. But whatever your family situation, home is a place where you should be cared for and where you feel secure and safe.

BULLIED BY A SIBLING

If you are being bullied at home by a sibling, you should tell a trusted adult—this could mean a parent, another relative, a teacher, or someone at your church or temple.

Talking to a grandparent or another relative can help if there is trouble at home, particularly if you are an only child.

BULLIED BY AN ADULT

Sometimes it might be a parent or another adult who is being the bully. An adult has a right to **discipline** you, but no one, including a parent or teacher, has the right to hurt you physically or mentally, to injure you, abuse you, or neglect you. If you're not sure if what you're experiencing is bullying or not, or what to do, phone a helpline about it.

Under Pressure Q&A

My stepmom doesn't want me—what can I do?

My dad has married his girlfriend, so now I have a stepmom. In front of Dad, she's really nice to me, but when he isn't there, she turns all sarcastic and mocking. She keeps dropping hints that soon they'll have their own children and there won't be any room for me. I can't stay with my mom, and I don't have anywhere else to go. Dad won't listen—what can I do?

No one should make you feel that way, especially the adults who are supposed to be caring for you. Is there a member of the family you can speak to, such as an aunt or grandparent? Or a teacher you really trust? If not, try Childhelp or another helpline and they will be able to talk it through with you.

SIGNS OF BULLYING

Sometimes people who are being bullied are so ashamed that they don't want anyone to know. They may think they are weak and worthless and feel too scared to tell anyone. Their fear, anger, and shame are kept inside but can show themselves in harmful ways.

WITHDRAWN AND SICK

If someone is being bullied, he or she may start to become very withdrawn and want to spend more and more time alone. He or she might start missing school, perhaps using a headache or stomachache as an excuse. These are signs that the person could be depressed, and in extreme cases, this could lead to thoughts of suicide.

If there is no one you can turn to at home or school, try phoning a helpline. There will always be someone there to give you advice and encouragement.

ASK TO TALK

If someone close to you seems sad, angry, withdrawn, or anxious all the time, ask what's bothering them. Let them know you're there for them and that whatever the problem, you won't think any less of them. If you're really concerned, talk to an adult—you could be saving that person from a dangerous situation.

SELF-HARMING

Some young people who are bullied may feel angry, scared, and ashamed but feel unable to talk about these bad feelings. They bottle up their emotions and may resort to self-harming as a way of releasing their negative feelings.

GET HELP

If you are self-harming or know someone who is, you should try to talk to an adult about it. The Childhelp website has some ideas for coping techniques to help stop self-harming.

Offering support to a person being bullied can help her or him get through the bad times.

Under Pressure Q&A

How can I help my best friend?

My best friend has started missing school. When he does come, he always looks scared. I saw he had a bruise on his arm, and when I asked him about it, he got really angry and told me to leave him alone. How can I help him?

Your friend sounds like he's going through a hard time, and it's great he's got you looking out for him. Try and talk to him again about what's going on. It could be trouble at home or bullies at school. If he gets angry, it's probably because he's scared and ashamed. Send him a text message or email suggesting he try a helpline and just letting him know that you're there to help. Also talk to a teacher, parent, or counselor about it—or you can phone a helpline to get some advice about how to help your friend.

HOW TO STOP BEING A BULLY

Are you bullying someone? Hurting other people in any way is wrong, and being a bully can get you into lots of trouble. Ask a teacher or an adult you trust, or phone a helpline for advice on how to stop bullying—you'll get lots of support.

It takes more courage to ask for help to stop bullying than it does to bully.

STOP AND THINK

Some bullies don't realize what they're doing is hurting someone. The person you are teasing or making jokes about may laugh, but this could be because they don't want to be a "wimp." If the joke was turned on you, how would you feel? If you're a bully who was bullied, think about how bad it made you feel and how much you hated the person who bullied you. Do you really want others to feel like that about you?

SAY YOU'RE SORRY

To change your behavior, apologize to those you are bullying or have bullied. Say you want to be friends. They may not trust you right away, but just start being nice to them, or at least stop being nasty and leave them alone.

Deliberately leaving someone out of your group can make him or her feel very lonely—talk to that person today and explain the bullying is over.

FEELING ANGRY?

Some bullies have trouble controlling their feelings. If you feel angry a lot, talk to a teacher, school counselor, or an adult you trust. They will be glad that you are trying to change your behavior and will give you all the help they can. Or you can phone a helpline for advice.

"It made me feel big"

I was the youngest kid at home in a big family, and my brothers and sisters were always picking on me. Mom and Dad said I had to stick up for myself. I guess it made me feel important when I started bullying little kids at school—it made me feel I was getting my own back for being bullied at home. Then one day, I saw one of the kids crying in a corner in the playground—that was how I used to feel at home. I said sorry, and now I've stopped bullying, but I still need to deal with stuff at home.

PEER PRESSURE

Your peers are people who are close to you in age and have similar experiences and interests. If you belong to a club or group, the others involved in the same activity are your peers. Peers are people you identify with and like and admire.

GROUP OF FRIENDS

Everyone likes to feel that they "belong" to a group that they share things with and that they feel safe with. Our first "group" is our family. At school, we make yet another "group"—friends. This group of friends, our peers, is very important to us.

PEER POWER

The peers we mix with at school might become our friends for life, but peers also have the power to make us feel very bad or to make us do things we don't want to.

PUTTING ON THE PRESSURE

Our peers can influence us to behave in certain ways—this is called peer pressure. It can be positive—peers can encourage you to take up exciting new activities. It can also be negative—your peers might try to convince you to join in harmful activities and threaten to isolate you if you refuse to take part.

Shopping, chatting, and going for a snack after school are all great ways to spend time with your peers.

Do you think real friends would try and make you do things that are dangerous or illegal?

STAND UP TO PEER PRESSURE

If your friends ask you to do something you don't want to, politely say no. It's hard, but you will feel better for refusing. Explain why you don't want to. If they insist, say you'll get into trouble at home or make an excuse, for example, that you don't feel well. If they still insist, walk away.

Under Pressure Q&A

Should I join in?

My friends have started picking on a new girl at school. She's a bit geeky but OK. I don't like to call her names, but they just laugh and say it's fun. I'm scared that if I don't join in, they'll start picking on me or leave me out.

Bullying is never, ever fun for the person being bullied, and name-calling can be really hurtful. Your friends are putting pressure on you to do something you don't want to do. Say you feel uncomfortable about name-calling and that you have some research or homework to do instead. Your friends sound like bullies. Try to convince them to stop teasing the girl or think about joining another group.

DON'T BE A BYSTANDER

You may think that because you are not sending nasty text messages, calling people names, or pushing them, you are not involved in bullying. However, if you ignore the situation, you're allowing the bullying to continue.

Sit with someone who is being bullied and left out—it will make him or her feel better and more able to deal with the bullying.

DON'T JUST WATCH

Bullies enjoy attention, so if you stand around and watch them bully someone, this will encourage them to do it more. Also, knowing people are watching and doing nothing to help is humiliating for the person being bullied and adds to his or her feeling of being worthless.

BE A LIFESAVER

People who are being bullied can feel lonely and isolated. Someone standing up for them could be a lifesaver. If you know someone who is being bullied, sit next to him or her at lunch or talk to him or her at recess, so the bullies can see that person is not alone.

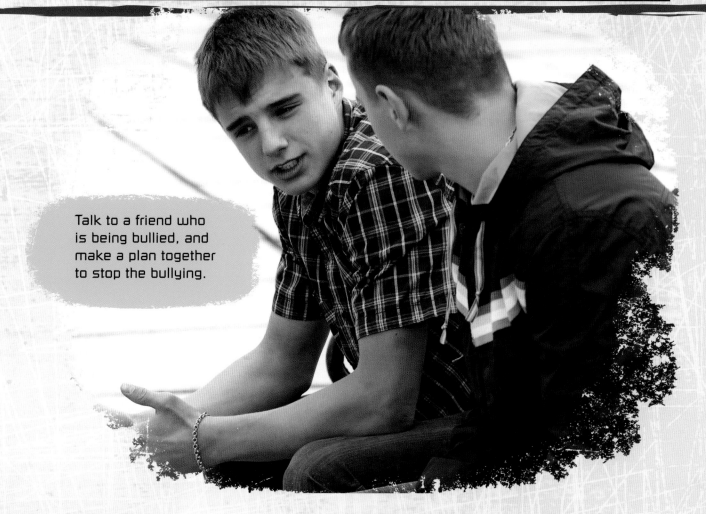

Talk to a friend who is being bullied, and make a plan together to stop the bullying.

WALK TOGETHER

If the person is being bullied outside of school, see if you can walk to the bus stop or train station with him or her. Just having someone there will give the person being bullied the confidence to act and be stronger.

NO BULLIES HERE!

If people don't stand up to bullies, they will continue doing it and the bullying could get worse. Start an antibullying group or club to make your school a bully-free zone. Remember, if you do nothing, you give the bullies more power.

"I couldn't have done it without her"

The bullies used to call me names and shove me and knock my things over. People would watch or walk by like it wasn't happening. I thought, "Am I invisible or something?" Then one day, this girl came over who was a grade above me and said to the bullies: "Stop! Just stop bullying this girl. She doesn't deserve it! What if someone did that to you?" She helped me up, and the bullies just shrugged and walked off. She took me to see the principal and helped me to talk about it. I couldn't have done it without her help. Now I try to keep an eye out for others being bullied.

TYPES OF GANGS

There are different types of gangs. Sometimes close-knit groups of school friends call themselves "gangs." Some school gangs bully people, but most don't. Criminal gangs are vicious and are often involved in violent and illegal behavior.

WHY DO PEOPLE JOIN GANGS?

People join gangs for lots of reasons. It feels safe and secure to be part of a group or maybe they all have a lot in common or like the same things. Some people might join bullying gangs because they are afraid that they might become the target for bullying otherwise.

SCHOOL GANGS

Hanging out with your friends is OK if you're not hurting or scaring anyone else. Being part of a group means you can look out for each other. But gangs can become a problem if they start to bully or threaten others.

Making new friends at an after-school group will help you to break away from a bullying gang.

Choose friends who help you to relax and be yourself.

BULLYING GANGS

If you belong to a gang that has started to bully someone, it can be really hard to stand up and say they shouldn't do it. Try to convince them to stop—but if they don't, refuse to participate. See if you can find another group, or try a new sport or activity and make some different friends.

Under Pressure Q&A

I can't leave or they'll turn on me ...

My gang was really fun, but one girl started saying nasty things about her ex-best friend and now the rest have joined in. They're sending her mean texts, have told everyone not to talk to her, and they're starting to follow her home and make threats. I don't want to be part of it, but I can't leave—or they'll turn on me, too.

It's great that you don't want to be part of the bullying. You should try to talk to an adult—a teacher or counselor—at school about this. The school should know what is going on and take steps to stop it. It is illegal to make threats of violence, and the longer this goes on, the more likely it is to become a matter for the police. What about the other girls in the group? Maybe they're just all going along with it because they're scared, too? Talk to each one separately and see if you can get them to leave the gang— if the leader is isolated, she'll soon stop.

CRIMINAL GANGS

Some gangs, especially outside of school, can be violent, carry weapons such as knives, and deal in drugs. They will often have adult members but might try and recruit young members from school. You should avoid these kinds of gangs at any cost.

WHY DO PEOPLE JOIN CRIMINAL GANGS?

Young people might feel that a criminal gang will look after them and give them the confidence to stand up to people. They may think it is exciting to join a gang, and maybe they think that they will make a lot of money. But being part of a criminal gang can put you in a lot of personal danger and get you into trouble with the police.

SIGNS OF LOYALTY

Many criminal gangs expect members to get tattoos or wear certain types of shoes or clothes, so that others know which gang they belong to. To prove your loyalty, they might ask you to do something illegal, such as attacking someone, damaging property, or stealing.

Some violent street gangs use knives to threaten, injure, and even kill rival gang members or gang "enemies."

PEER PRESSURE

Sometimes people feel that they are forced into gang membership by peer pressure. Maybe a friend is already a member, or someone says how cool it is to be in a gang. They may say that everyone is doing it and that you're a loser if you're not in a gang.

"Worst thing I ever did"

I was bored so I joined a gang. Worst thing I ever did. Joining a gang affected my life really badly, to the point where I didn't care about my family or what they wanted. It was all about me and what I wanted to do. We would terrorize people and smash up their property. It was such a rush at the time, and it felt daring. But now I feel terrible about being part of it. I managed to get out of the gang with the help of my family, but I still have to avoid gang members. It scares me that they might try and get me to go back, but I hope I'll know better next time.

Some gang members dress in a certain way as a "badge" to let others know which gang they belong to.

STAYING AWAY FROM CRIMINAL GANGS

In some places, gangs hang around the school gates hoping to pressure young people into joining them. For some younger people, gang life might seem attractive, but look at the problems older gang members have! They find it hard to get a job, nobody trusts them, sometimes their families are threatened, and many are in and out of prison.

Gangs sometimes target young people who are lonely or unhappy.

HANGING AROUND

Gang members will pick on people they see hanging around, doing nothing, and looking lost. They hang around street corners, parks, and skateparks and start talking to young people, then they start putting pressure on them to join the gang.

A FIRM "NO"

If some gang members start talking to you, be polite but don't get caught up in conversation with them. Stick with your own friends. If the gang members ask you to hang out with them, say that you're cool and that you won't get into any gangs.

Looking scary and threatening helps gangs to intimidate people.

NOT GLAMOROUS

Gang leaders will try and tell you how glamorous or exciting being part of a gang is—but it isn't! Mostly they just hang around street corners annoying or upsetting other people—what's the point of that? In extreme cases, gang members end up in prison or seriously hurt.

Under Pressure Q&A

How can I help my brother?

My brother has just started hanging around with this local gang. They are real troublemakers. I've tried to talk to my brother, but he tells me to mind my own business. Now the gang members have started telling me to leave him alone, and they are beginning to threaten me. They say they're his family now. Should I tell Mom or Dad? What if the gang finds out?

You should let an adult know what your brother is doing, or he could end up in serious trouble. Talk to your parents or maybe a teacher you trust at school. It is wise not to get involved with the gang members or talk to them yourself.

41

BE STRONG, BE CONFIDENT, BE YOU

No one deserves to be bullied, and there is never, ever a reason to bully anyone. Every one of us is special and important and deserves to be respected and to give respect. We all have the right to feel safe at home and at school and the responsibility to help others feel safe.

Look out for others at school and outside school to stop the bullies.

YOU ARE SPECIAL
Bullying can make someone feel small and worthless, but every single person is special and important. Respect your own worth as a person. Every day, think about something that is great about you or makes you happy—a skill you have, a person you love, a favorite book or place, a special memory. These are the things that make you yourself, not what the bullies say or do.

BE CONFIDENT
If bullies call you names, ignore them and say the opposite to yourself as you walk away. So, if they say you are stupid, say to yourself, "Of course, I'm not stupid. You have no idea how smart I am." Or keep saying, "I respect myself too much to let them get to me." Respecting yourself will help give you the strength and confidence to ask for help.

DON'T LET THE BULLIES WIN

Walk tall, be strong, and don't let the bullies win. If you see someone being bullied, stand up for him or her. If you are a bully, think about what you're doing, and decide to change your behavior. Can you really respect yourself when you are hurting others?

"I am a stronger person now"

I've always been a little shy, and at school, I was bullied by a gang that stole my lunch money, sent me nasty text messages, said horrible things about my family, and turned my friends against me. I was too scared to tell anyone. I felt like no one cared about me. It got so bad that I thought about running away, but I couldn't do it. So I tried a helpline, and they gave me some great advice and lots of support. They made me feel like I was worth something again. Eventually, I talked to my mom. We went to the school, and they were really supportive and helpful. I stood up to the bullies, and it's gotten a lot better. I still keep out of their way, but I am a stronger person now. I have more confidence in who I am. I respect myself and my right to be safe.

Be proud of who you are, and let others know that you will not tolerate bullying or unkind behavior—to yourself or to others.

GLOSSARY

aggressive Hostile, violent, or threatening.

anonymously The act of doing something—writing a letter, posting a comment or tweeting, for instance—without saying who you are.

antisocial Behaving in a manner that is harmful or annoying to other people or to society in general.

anxious Being afraid or nervous about something that might happen and your ability to cope with it.

assertive Confident and ready to stand up for your rights and beliefs.

bystanders People who watch an event but do not actively take part.

depression A mental state marked by sadness, inactivity, and lack of self-esteem.

discipline To train you to follow rules and ways to behave that are set by your family or school.

foster family A family that looks after a child who cannot be cared for by his or her birth parents.

harassment Annoying or worrying somebody by putting pressure on them or saying or doing unpleasant things to them.

hate crime A violent crime that is committed out of hatred for someone's race, skin color, sex, or sexual orientation.

humiliates Makes someone feel stupid and ashamed, especially in front of other people.

illegal Against the law.

inadequate Not capable of doing something properly.

intimidate Frighten someone by being threatening, aggressive, and/or violent.

passive Accepting what other people do or decide without trying to change anything.

prejudice A feeling of dislike against a person or group because of opinions about them that are not based on the facts.

procedures Rules and ways of doing things.

racist Disliking people or treating them unfairly because they belong to a different race.

reckless Showing a lack of care about danger and the possible results of your actions.

right Something that everyone has by law, such as the right to be safe, the right to have enough to eat, and the right to go to school.

self-esteem A person's belief in his or her own worth and abilities.

snitching Telling on someone, especially to people in charge or the police.

stepfamily A family that is formed when a parent marries a new partner who already has children.

transgender Used to describe someone who feels he or she should have been born the opposite gender, so a boy feels like he should be a girl, and a girl feels like she should be a boy.

WEB SITES

http://www.childhelp.org
Help and advice about bullying by other pupils and teachers. Includes games, videos, message boards, and chat rooms.

http://www.kidshealth.org/teen
A great website that covers a wide range of problems faced by young people, including bullying and peer pressure.

http://www.pacer.org/bullying/
The PACER National Bullying Prevention Center web site has lots of advice and information on bullying and what to do about it. Includes ideos made by young people talking about their experiences.

http://www.nsteens.org/
This web site has videos and information to help young people make safe choices online, with advice about cyberbullying.

http://www.stopbullying.gov
A U.S. government web site that offers lots of practical advice about bullying and how to get help. It also describes the laws on bullying for each state.

HELPLINES

Childhelp 1-800-422-4453 www.childhelp.org.

Samariteens 1-800-252-8336 www.samaritanshope.org

BOOKS

Bullies, Bigmouths and So-Called Friends by Jenny Alexander (Hodder & Stoughton, 2006)

The Bullying Workbook for Teens by Haley Kilpatrick, Raychelle Cassada Lohmann, and Julia V. Taylor (Instant Help, 2013)

Bystander Power: Now with Anti-Bullying Action by Phyllis Kaufman Goodstein and Elizabeth Verdick (Free Spirit Publishing, 2012)

INDEX